dedicated to:

....

....

....

celebrating

Weddings

share, remember, cherish

JIM McCANN, FOUNDER

**Andrews McMeel
Publishing, LLC**

Kansas City • Sydney • London

Andrews McMeel Publishing, LLC
an Andrews McMeel Universal company
1130 Walnut Street, Kansas City, Missouri 64106

www.andrewsmcmeel.com

12 13 14 15 16 SMA 10 9 8 7 6 5 4 3 2 1

ISBN: 978-1-4494-0981-4

Library of Congress Control Number: 2011932636

ATTENTION: SCHOOLS AND BUSINESSES
Andrews McMeel books are available at quantity discounts with bulk purchase for
educational, business, or sales promotional use. For information, e-mail the Andrews
McMeel Publishing Special Sales Department: specialsales@amuniversal.com

Project Manager and Editor: Heidi Tyline King

Designed by Alexis Siroc

Produced by SMALLWOOD & STEWART, INC., NEW YORK CITY

Illustration credit information on page 70.

introduction

WHEN MARYLOU AND I GOT MARRIED, I wanted to do something special for our wedding, so I decided to write my own vows. Full of nervous excitement on the day of the ceremony, I managed to get every word out, along with a few extra lines—and in a humble-jumble order that was not at all related to the original way I had written them. It was a little embarrassing at the time, but now, thirty-eight years later, remembering makes the two of us smile.

What could have been a sore subject has become our special memory, and it's a good example of how having the right perspective is key when it comes to your wedding day. I've witnessed just about every wedding fiasco you could imagine, from no-show caterers and last-minute reception hall cancellations to wedding dress mix-ups and members of the bridal party who took the "party" part a little too far. But no matter how terribly the big day played out, the couples who learned to roll with the punches seemed to be the ones who ended up being able to look back with a smile.

It's also interesting that, of all the weddings I've attended or arranged flowers for, the ones that stand out are those that were infused with the couple's personality. Not coincidentally, they were also the weddings at which the bride and groom clearly had the most fun! One couple we know, who were both passionate about the arts, turned the catering hall into an art museum with framed floral arrangements on the walls and ice sculptures on the buffet. Another couple with matching sweet tooths created an elaborate Candy Land theme, complete with mountains of colorful confections and waitstaff dressed in "Oompa Loompa" costumes. So go ahead with your dream of a *Gone With the Wind* theme, or rent a tux for your beloved golden retriever and include him in your ceremony. Sure, it's not conventional, but your guests will appreciate your personal flair and be honored to celebrate your uniqueness as a couple.

It's natural to want everything to go off without a hitch, but remember that all the little details make a wedding—not a marriage. The time for fixating on programs and bridesmaids' shoes has passed, and truthfully, the day goes by so fast that you're going to remember only a fraction of what happens. Make your wedding day all about the two of you beginning your life together, and the glorious blessing of getting to do so while basking in the love of family and friends.

And finally, I think it's important to take your vows seriously. If I've learned one thing from nearly forty years of marriage, it's that both of you will change—it's just that it rarely happens at the same time. You grow apart, then grow together. Love ebbs, then flows. There will be peaks and valleys, and they won't run concurrently. Being committed means that when one of you is flighty, the other one stands firmly grounded, holding the kite strings. It's not the easy way out, but it has the best reward: growing old together. I might have mixed up a few lines when I recited my vows those many years ago, but no matter their order, I meant every word.

will you MARRY ME?

Though you be two that love,
let there be one heart between you.

—ITALIAN PROVERB

When I worked at the party store, an elderly couple came into the store. I assumed they wanted to order fiftieth wedding anniversary invitations, but no. They were getting married. She was seventy, he was seventy-two, and this was the first marriage for each of them. I was stunned. As I helped them decide on the details, the man asked if I was married. "No, sir," I said.

"Well, you are young, and you have plenty of time," he said. "It took me seventy-two years to find her, so don't give up!" —CHARITY M.

Tradition has it that in the eighteenth century, a Dutch woman fell in love with a poor miller. Her father refused to allow the marriage, concerned that she would live a future in poverty. So friends and neighbors "showered" the young woman with everything she would need.

*He encourages me, challenges me,
and makes me want to be a better person.
He fights for me and prays for me.
He brings out the best in me,
and he loves me despite my flaws.
He makes my heart sing.*

—VICTORIA H.

I dreamed of a wedding of elaborate elegance:

a church filled with flowers and friends.

I asked him what kind of wedding he wished for:

he said one that would make me his wife.

—ANONYMOUS

It's so easy for brides to get caught up with trying to
plan the perfect day. But even in the craziness, try
to remember what it's all about: marrying the perfect
guy. This thought grounds you and ensures that,
no matter what happens, your celebration will be
amazing and full of love. —MELISSA B.

*M*y one piece of advice for brides-to-be is to include your friends and family in your wedding, no matter how small or what future celebratory plans you think you might have. After marrying at the justice of the peace, my husband and I had planned to have a wedding reception once he returned from his deployment to Afghanistan. The economy, however, put that plan on hold. So now, while I have no regrets about marrying him, I do regret that we didn't invite everyone down to the courthouse to share in our special day! —JAIMIE N.

It is better to know as little as possible
of the defects of the person with whom you
are to pass your life.

—JANE AUSTEN

Don't try to make
everyone else happy—
it's your wedding!

—BRIGITTE K.

Four days after we met, Justin told me,

"I will marry you someday."

It took three years, but he made good on his promise!

—JENNA H.

My mom, who has, for better or worse,
been married five times, always says,
"Have at least one marriage
with someone who enjoys life!"

—CYNDY D.

American brides typically choose a diamond for their engagement ring, but why not add significance by choosing your favorite gemstone or one with personal meaning? Among your choices:

Emerald: *love and rebirth*

Sapphire: *sincerity and fidelity*

Amethyst: **protection and tranquility**

Opal: *hope and purity*

Aquamarine: *a long, successful marriage*

Jade: *royalty and love*

Turquoise: *creative force*

Pearl: *modesty, purity, and a happy marriage*

Diamond: *pure and unbreakable love*

With this ring...

It's not about the bling ... wedding rings actually carry great significance for a wedding couple:

- A ring's circular shape symbolizes eternal love, wholeness, and completion.

- It was once believed that the *vena amoris*, the vein of love, ran directly from the heart to the third finger of the left hand, hence the tradition.

- Ancient couples exchanged rings made of hemp or braided grass. Early Romans used iron, a more durable symbol. Egyptian rings were gold to symbolize the groom's wealth and intention to wed.

- Platinum, the strongest metal, is associated with heaven. Incredibly rare and pure, it is the perfect metaphor for love.

We had "met" on the Internet, then decided to officially meet on a blind date at the beach. Four hours turned into three years, love, and a proposal! —LISA R.

Everyone knows the Bible verse about not letting the sun set on your anger. Well, my grandparents would always tease each other about it. My grandmother would tell us, "Never go to bed mad," to which my grandfather, with a twinkle in his eye, would reply, "That's why I've been awake since 1942!" —CLAYTON C.

On our second date, my future wife
lit her hair on fire.
As the smell of burnt hair wafted
around us, all we could do was laugh.
The rest is history.

—JOHN L.

will you marry me?

When we decided to marry, it was only fitting to return to our "special place," the beach. My favorite picture was taken at midnight, the two of us in our wedding attire, sitting at the table where we had met three years before. —LISA R.

blessings

To have and to hold
from this day forward,
for better or worse,
for richer for poorer,
in sickness and in health,
to love and to cherish
to death do us part.

—BOOK OF COMMON PRAYER

My wedding stylist had just finished curling my hair when she said, "Wow, I can't believe how calm you are!" She was right: There wasn't an anxious nerve in my body—or in my heart. But was there supposed to be? Was I supposed to feel scared or worried about the years ahead? Was I supposed to second-guess everything because the florist made the wrong bouquet? If the answer to any of these questions was yes, apparently I missed the memo. My heart was at peace; I was confident, and I was ready. —VICTORIA H.

When we walked into the reception after

our wedding, we were greeted with the loudest

cheers I've ever heard. It was like being at a

ballgame with the entire crowd rooting for us.

Their shouts of support gave us confidence

that we were, indeed, going to have

a successful life together.

— ANTHONETTE K.

During our ceremony, my husband accidentally blew out our unity candle, and our guests erupted in laughter. Some would consider this bad luck, but nearly ten years later, we are still married—and still laughing. —JULIA C.

The favorite part of my wedding?
The fact that my seven-year-old daughter signed
our wedding license as a witness!

—CHRISTINA P.

Make sure to include family *and* friends

in your wedding ceremony and reception so that it's as personal

and meaningful as possible. We wouldn't be the couple

we were without their wonderful influence.

—HANNAH D.

Our wedding was wonderful.

Two hundred friends and family joined us in our backyard, and my bride's seven grandchildren gave her away. When the preacher asked, "Who gives this woman?" they all shouted simultaneously, "We do!" —TIM C.

When Kate Middleton married Prince William,

she chose a royal bouquet with flowers of significance

for both the royal and Middleton families.

These included lily of the valley (return of happiness),

sweet William (gallantry), hyacinth (constancy of love),

ivy (fidelity, marriage, affection), and

myrtle (emblem of marriage and tradition

stemming from Queen Victoria's bridal bouquet

in the ninteenth century).

Floriology:
The Language of Flowers

Amaryllis ⌒ splendid beauty, pride

Baby's breath ⌒ fruitful marriage

Bluebell ⌒ constancy

Calla lily ⌒ magnificent beauty

Camellia ⌒ perfect loveliness

Carnation ⌒ strong love, beauty

Daisy ⌒ innocence

Fern ⌒ earnestness

Forsythia ⌒ anticipation

Hibiscus ⁀ delicate beauty

Honeysuckle ⁀ bonds of love

Jasmine ⁀ joy, grace

Lilac ⁀ first love

Orange blossoms ⁀ purity, good luck

Orchid ⁀ beauty, love

Rose ⁀ love, beauty, desire

Rosemary ⁀ remembrance, fidelity, loyalty

Roses ⁀ the ultimate bloom of love

Stephanotis ⁀ happiness

Sweet pea ⁀ lasting pleasure

Tulip ⁀ true love

Wheat ⁀ fertility, prosperity

Something old,
Something new,
Something borrowed,
Something blue...
And a silver sixpence in her shoe.

Many of the weddings I've attended have focused on the sanctity of marriage rather than messages of love or sharing stories about the wedding couple. My friend's wedding was quite different.

During the nuptials, the rabbi contradicted the adage that marriage symbolizes two people becoming one and instead emphasized that marriage means that you found the person who makes you the very best version of yourself and supports you to reach your individual dreams throughout life's ups and downs.

Recently engaged, I am fortunate to say that I have found my special person. He pushes me to challenge myself, and encourages me to be patient when my goals seem out of reach. I look forward to us helping each other become the best form of ourselves and sharing the rabbi's message at our own ceremony to inspire others. —SHARMY N.

It was important to me that our wedding truly be "our wedding," so in all the planning that I did, I tried to incorporate symbolism or personal significance. We wrote our own ketubah for the rabbi to use. We had our rings engraved. And we even used our own wording for the invitations, much to the chagrin of the printer. I knew that everything was going to work out just fine when she exclaimed, "But you can't say that—it wouldn't be simple, sophisticated, and elegant!" —LISA R.

My wedding was all kinds of perfect. The special touch
was the butterflies we released at the end of our ceremony—
just gorgeous! It's something that my wife and
all of our guests will remember forever.

—JON N.

Old Wives' Tales

- A bride who sews the last few stitches of her gown makes her happiness complete.

- Listen to the bird calls on your wedding day. A singing wren is lucky; a raven call signals that you will know poverty.

- Ancient superstition holds that demons fear leather; that's why shoes are tied to the back bumper of the newlyweds' car.

- A marriage made when the tide is coming in will prosper.

- Weepy brides take note: tears before the vows are a good thing; they mean no crying after.

n sixteenth-century France, a small piece of bread was always placed in the bottom of a wineglass to soak up the sediment. The last person to drink from the glass got the "toast"— and a dose of good luck.

*Let there be spaces
in your togetherness.*

—KHALIL GIBRAN

So what if I had to jump over a
mud puddle to get to the altar;
I get to spend the rest of my life
with my best friend!

—LACY K.

THREE

HERE COMES
THE *bride*

More than yesterday,
less than tomorrow....

—ANONYMOUS

Do everything together and
stay together at your reception.
That way you will enjoy
the evening as one forever.

—GARY M.

There had been one mishap after the next, but the week before my wedding, everything that could go wrong did. I learned that my baker had quit and left the country. When we picked up our rings, we realized that the jeweler has misread the inscription, so instead of my husband's ring saying, "Love H," it read, "Love TT."

I couldn't wait until it was all over.

But the second I put my white dress on and saw my husband's face for the first time, it was obvious that the real love was going to last way longer than all the wedding hype. —HANNAH D.

I married with one word in mind:
forever.

—ANTHONETTE K.

You could say my wedding was a "hopping good time!" That's because a few nights before we said, "I do," my husband was in a minor motorcycle accident. During the ceremony, he couldn't stand on one of his legs, so he literally hopped in place while reciting his vows! —CHRISTINA P.

My husband is not fond of crowds, so we planned a small ceremony with only seven people, including the pastor. Even then, Jim was nervous. When the pastor was almost to the point where we recite our vows, Jim, in his anxiousness, quickly said, "I do." The pastor, chuckling, said, "Not yet, Jim." He continued, pausing when he reached the point for Jim to speak. Jim said nothing. "Now, Jim," the pastor said, chuckling once again. "Yeah, okay," Jim said. We all laughed. To this day, I tell people our official vows were "I do" and "Yeah, okay." —LINDA P.

THE LONGEST WEDDING TRAIN WAS 670 FEET.
IT WAS WORN BY HEGE LORENCE IN
NORWAY IN 1996, AND REQUIRED 186 BRIDESMAIDS
AND PAGEBOYS TO CARRY IT.

before our marriage

(the second for both of us), my husband and I were saving every penny for the wedding and honeymoon. However, his rent kept going up, so we decided to move in together. The only issue was that we wanted to set a good example for our three teenage daughters by getting married before we moved in together. So, after work one afternoon, with all three daughters in tow, we ran down to our pastor's office and got married! Jim moved in that evening, and we both went to work the next day as if nothing had happened. A few months later, we had our big wedding, and most of the guests were none the wiser. In a sense, we got two weddings for the price of one, and each year, when Jim forgets which anniversary to celebrate, I always tell him, "BOTH!"

—STACY S.

While walking down the aisle, I realized that I had forgotten to pull my veil down over my face. My sweet dad stopped in an attempt to make amends. As he fumbled with the lace, laughter rippled through the church, breaking the tension in an emotional but lighthearted way.

—AMANDA T.

Getting married at the courthouse wasn't the most romantic option, but it sure was the most memorable. After a whirlwind romance, my husband and I decided to tie the knot before he deployed for Afghanistan. However, he had no vacation time, and his supervisor wouldn't grant him a few hours off work. Lunch hour was our only option. We dashed to the courthouse, which is also the county jail. There, we said our vows with the inmates looking on, posed for our photographer, the bailiff, in front of the copier, and then celebrated with a reception at Subway. My husband was deployed fourteen days later, so there was no honeymoon. Still, I'd do it all over again. It's not the ceremony that matters; it's who you marry. And I married the most caring, loving, generous man I have ever met. —LEAH S.

One of the more touching wedding ceremonies I have ever had the pleasure of attending was held in a New York City public park, where folding chairs were set up in the midst of families playing and couples walking along the stone paths. The groom and groomsmen wore Converse sneakers; the bride was gorgeous in one of the most breathtaking lace gowns I've ever seen.

While the setting was breathtaking in its ease and elegance, even more perfect were the words spoken by the bride and groom. As they shared stories of a young love, how they met, and the highlights of their eight-year relationship, tears welled up in each guest's eyes. It's amazing how a wedding can make even grown men cry! —ERIN S.

PARIS 1957. I had sailed over to visit my beau,

and we decided to marry. However, it took five months just to get documents and clearance from the U.S. government since Lawrence was in the counterintelligence corps. When the day arrived, a tiny, graybearded mayor wearing a sash emblazoned with the red, white, and blue French flag leaned forward and said, "Etes-vous, Gwen?"

"Oui," I said.

"Etes-vous, Lawrence?"

"Oui," he said.

We ad-libbed a few more lines, and exchanged rings. That was it—two minutes, tops! —GWEN R.

When you meet someone who can cook and do housework— don't hesitate—marry him.

—ANONYMOUS

just before our ceremony began, my one and only bridesmaid ripped her dress. Wouldn't you know, my mom just happened to have a sewing kit with the exact color of dusty-plum thread. Mom has always been more prepared than a Boy Scout, and this time she came through when it really mattered! —ANTHONETTE K.

Pour your time and effort into the ceremony. Everyone thinks ahead to the reception, but the wedding is the most important event of the day~ it's what will last and sustain you.

—DAVE L.

here comes the bride

my bouquet was wrapped in lace from my mother's wedding gown. I wore the same pearls my grandmother did on her wedding day. And we placed a guitar at the front of the church in memory of my husband's late father. You can keep all of the traditional elements of a wedding, but it's crucial to slip in pieces of yourselves if you want to make the ceremony meaningful. We still have people telling us that it was the best wedding they had ever attended!

—HANNAH D.

many underestimate the power of feeling at peace, but its significance on our wedding day was inspiring. Even though there was no time for my bridal portraits, the flowers were different than expected, and our siblings were late to the reception, my peaceful heart remained constant. Nothing mattered, because I would soon be united with my best friend; side by side, hip to hip, till death do we part. I wanted nothing more than to be his wife and share adventures with him for the rest of our lives. —VICTORIA H.

Weddings Around the World

- In the Middle East, the bitter herb artemisia is incorporated into bridal bouquets to ensure that marriages will survive bitterness as well as sweetness.

- In traditional Greek Orthodox weddings, crowns of orange blossoms were made for the bride and groom—they even matched the delicate embroidery on the bride's dress.

- In Thailand, the mothers of the bride and groom walk to the altar to drape puang malai, or flower garlands, around the couple's shoulders to wish them good fortune in their life together.

- Brides in Tudor England carried marigolds dipped in rosewater, and then ate them afterward, since they were thought to be aphrodisiacs!

- In Italy, the front of the getaway car is decorated with flowers, paving the road to a happy marriage.

je t'aime
te quiero saranghe
amo-te ♡ ia tibia lioubliou
mon amour je t'aime ti amo
ich liebe dich
wo ai ni te iubesc
TE AMO I love you *love*
ti amo jag älskar dig
amour eg elska ig je t'aime
volim te
amo-te seni seviyorum
s'agapo ik houd van jou amo-te
LOVE saranghe ich liebe dich
seni seviyorum volim te te quiero
jeg elsker deg I love you
szeretlek je t'aime AMORE, aishitemasu
te iubesc eu te amo EG ELSKA IG
ich liebe dich ti amo je t'aime
I love you t'estimo *love*
SARANGHE amo-te
jeg elsker deg
wo ai ni
s'agapo
♡

l'úbim t'a
ia tibia lioubliou
amo-te JE T'AIME
love ich liebe dich ti amo
l'úbim t'a I love you wo ai ni
t'estimo jeg elsker dig
amo-te seni seviyorum
szeretlek ik houd van jou
miluji tě TE IUBESC
LOVE je t'aime amo-te
ti amo wo ai ni
I ♡ YOU

having been both blessed and cursed with waist-long, curly dark hair, my attempts to straighten it were usually in vain. So on the day of my rehearsal dinner, my fiancé's cousin trimmed it to a more manageable shoulder-length look. Unknown to me, however, was that the cousin thought it would be funny to give my future husband the locks that had been trimmed as an early wedding present.

That night at the rehearsal, my beloved didn't speak to me but spent the evening glaring in my direction. I went to sleep not knowing if he would say, "I do."

The next day, when my father and I proceeded down the aisle, I wept with relief when I saw my now husband turn and smile at me. It was the same grin and twinkle in his eye that I had fallen in love with when I first saw him at age sixteen! —LEILA T.

becoming HUSBAND AND *wife*

Whatever our souls are made of,
his and mine are the same.

—EMILY BRONTË

Peace is one of love's best companions.
Peace is proof of love.

—VICTORIA H.

*Marriage has many pains,
but celibacy has no pleasures.*

—SAMUEL JOHNSON

THERE IS NOTHING NOBLER OR MORE ADMIRABLE

THAN WHEN TWO PEOPLE WHO SEE EYE TO EYE

KEEP HOUSE AS MAN AND WIFE,

CONFOUNDING THEIR ENEMIES AND

DELIGHTING THEIR FRIENDS.

—HOMER

Love is friendship set on fire.

— BRIGITTE K.

When my husband, Franco, and I decided to marry, we eloped to New Mexico, where Bob, one of his friends and a federal magistrate, had agreed to marry us. Ironically, in that state a federal judge can't marry people, so he quickly found another judge to do the honors. He also invited a few more of his friends—all judges—to the ceremony. One officiated, one took the photos, and the others were witnesses. To say that our marriage is legal is an understatement! — GWEN R.

We had both been married before, and each of us had the big traditional wedding the first time around. Yet here we were, both divorced, in love, and ready to commit. Only one thing was stopping us—getting married!

After one emotionally charged discussion, it dawned on us: If getting married the "right way" didn't work out the first time, why put ourselves through that rigmarole again? So we ditched the big plans for a ceremony in our living room. Dressed in our favorite shirts and jeans and surrounded by my three children and a handful of family, we became husband and wife.

To make it all the more special, our wedding date was May 29, his parents' wedding anniversary date, and my youngest son's birthday.

Looking back, we have no regrets about the small ceremony—only a beautiful and happy family with three times the reason to celebrate a special day. —MAYRYA W.

The word "forever" is powerful for myself and my husband because we both have families extended many times over due to numerous divorces. Consequently, we are determined to make ours last forever. My husband and I are now going on year thirteen, and though we have a long time together ahead of us, we married ". . . till death do us part." —ANTHONETTE K.

A husband always prefers his wife's
mother-in-law to his own.

—ANONYMOUS

Marriage is three parts love and seven
parts forgiveness of sins.

—LAO TZU

Peace is proof of love.

—VICTORIA H.

To save money, I purchased thousands of crystal beads and hand sewed them to my dress. I like to think that each bead represents one day of happiness for us— and also a dollar saved! —BRIGITTE K.

What greater thing is there for two human souls, than to feel that they are joined for life— to strengthen each other in all labor, to rest on each other in all sorrow, to minister to each other in all pain, to be one with each other in silent unspeakable memories at the moment of the last parting? —GEORGE ELIOT

It started with an over-the-phone proposal and ended with guests skinny-dipping in the pool. Let's just say I'd change everything about my wedding… except the groom and the cake! —JENNA H.

A few weeks before our wedding, a lady showed up at my door. I knew her only by legend, a friend of the family. She was at least eighty, and dressed in pearls, a shirtdress, and pumps at nine in the morning—an elegant southern matron.

As I invited her in, she handed me a gift. Both obsessed with my impending wedding and intimidated by this legendary lady, I asked offhandedly, "How long have you been married?"

"Sixty-three years," she replied.

"Wow!" I said. "That's amazing. How did you and your husband accomplish such a long marriage?"

"Well, the first ten years were a little rough," she said in a matter-of-fact way.

The first ten years?

I could barely imagine the first ten days. But now, twenty-one years into our marriage, I completely get what she was saying. —ANN S.

A deaf husband and a blind wife are always a happy couple.

—DANISH PROVERB

I think a man and a woman should choose each other for life,

for the simple reason that a long life with all its accidents

is barely enough time for a man and a woman to understand

each other. To understand is to love.

—WILLIAM BUTLER YEATS

A happy marriage is a long conversation
which always seems too short.

—ANDRE MAUROIS